APR 8 8

 P9-AEX-446

RON ERRERA

With the outbreak of peace in 1945, the enormous but hitherto-dormant American automobile industry shook off the cobwebs of a four-year layoff and burst into life spurred by the unprecedented demands of a car hungry public. First models to roll off most of the production lines where new in little more than name; despite the modest styling changes, they were in reality dressed up 1942 cars. Lack of novelty, however, was not an immediate problem as showrooms were filled to overflowing, and the customers were queueing up outside.

But it was not only the giants, such as Chrysler, Ford and Chevrolet that were attempting to fill their order books. Newcomers, too, were elbowing their way into the act with mixed results. And if the earliest models were notable for their conservatism, then it was not long before automobile styling underwent a revolution that has marked the post-war period as one of the most exciting in the industry's history. In their attempt to come up with a styling leader, designers sought to interpret public taste, and in the process came up with some radical and audacious ideas. Cadillac's outrageous tail fin, which would later virtually become the company's trademark, made its first, tentative appearance in 1948, while Hudson opted for clean lines and absence of any unnecessary gimmicks. Packard, at the top end of the industry, came out with a slab-sided design that came in for a considerable amount of criticism but still managed to sell extremely well.

The year 1950 marked the beginnings of a period of overabundance in almost everything, and cars were no exception. Longer, lower, wider, faster seemed to be the aim as flamboyance suddenly became the keyword, and competition heated up to fever pitch. For those such as Crosley and Kaiser, as with Tucker some years earlier, the fever was to prove terminal. Crosley's economical four cylinder car was plagued with numerous problems and Kaiser's swan-song, the extraordinary Kaiser-Darrin, failed to capture the car-buying public's imagination. Ultimately, even better known names such as De Soto and Studebaker, whose stunning Avanti failed to live up to its promise, faded from the scene. Even giants like Ford, with their Edsel, showed how easily consumer demand could be misjudged.

On the positive side, however, were the longer-lived, successful models such as the Mustangs and Thunderbirds from Ford, the Riviera by Buick and the exciting Chevrolet Camaro. Also from Chevrolet, with design by the talented Bill Mitchell and engineered by Zora Duntov, came the fabulous Corvette Stingray; a fiberglass-bodied flyer that was guaranteed to turn heads wherever it appeared. It is these remarkable creations, as well as others like the memorable 1957 Chevrolet, Chrysler's 300 and the Ford Skyliner with its retractable hardtop, that are among the most notable of the period.

In an age of standardisation and rationalisation, of economics and ergonomics, car design seems to have lost much of its flair and pizazz, making us appreciate all the more the creations that graced the classic post-war era of American car production.

The Sedanet or Fastback styling theme had been used by Buick since 1941 and nowhere was it more attractive than on the 1949 Roadmaster Sedanet Model 76-S. New were the "portholes" on the front fenders, a styling gimmick that has remained a Buick trademark to this day. Note the massive over-riders on the front bumper; this was an optional feature probably designed for aggressive parking! This car belongs to the A-C-D Museum, Auburn, Ind.

The finest of wood and steel crafted automobiles, the Chrysler Town & Country was arguably the original personal luxury car; the toy of the Hollywood highflyers. This mint 1948 example belongs to T & C buff, Roy Bleeke of Fort Wayne, and shows how well the handcrafted wood sections blend into the body. Huge overriders set off the heavily chromed grille, behind which nestles Chrysler's C-39 Spitfire Straight Eight rated at 135 hp. The Town & Country came with most options as standard, including Chrysler's semi-automatic Fluid Drive transmission and leather upholstery. Total cost in 1948 was $3420. A cheaper version, a four door sedan on a shorter wheelbase, was also available.

Pictures *left and top* are of the Tucker, possibly the world's most advanced automobile in 1948. Only 50 were made before Preston Tucker's dream ended in the courts. Styled by Alex Tremulis and Egan, the Tucker was very radical for its day. More importantly, it was mechanically very advanced. It had a full safety cockpit, pop out windshield in the event of an accident and a rear mounted aluminium flat opposed air cooled Franklin six displacing 335 cu. ins. The front center light turned with the wheels and the simple, but massive, grille/bumper arrangement conducted air into the car interior. If that wasn't enough, the doors cut into the roof and the Tucker had four wheel independent suspension. The Tucker was America's chance to get out in front of everyone but she blew it! Pete Kesling owns this car which is on display at A-C-D museum.

▲ Brook Stevens, the well known designer, was contracted by Willys to design a sporty family version of the company's wartime Jeep. Stevens' design was unusual and quite attractive and the Jeepster, as it was called, did reasonably well with first year sales of 10,000 plus. Both the 1948 and 1949 models had the traditional upright jeep grille but the center section was chromed and capped by a winged motive giving the appearance of an Indian totem pole. Paula Kash's 1949 Jeepster has a 63 hp four under its hood and Mrs. Kash did most of the restoration herself.

The first Lincoln Continental met public acclaim in 1940. It had a V-12 displacing 292 ► cu. in. and produced 120 hp at 3500 rpm. 1942 models were extensively restyled at the front end and the pointed hood of 1940 was replaced by a coffin nosed one. 1946 to 1948 Lincolns and Continentals picked up where they left off when interrupted by the war. About the only change was the grille pattern which was divided into vertical and horizontal bars. The L-head V-12 had five extra horsepower, otherwise it remained the same. This Continental courtesy the A-C-D Museum, Auburn, Ind.

▲ If ever there was a car that spoke for the fifties' youth then it has to be the 1949 – '51 Mercury. Its high waistline, rounded curves and narrow glass area begged customizing and its 255.4 cid L-head V-8 had enough guts for cruisin' down the boulevard on hot summer's nights. More often than not customizers dispensed with the sliced sausage grille for something much wilder and chopped the low roofline even lower. And the

◄ Kaiser-Frazer wasn't doing too well by 1949 and a new small car was proposed by Henry J. Kaiser to help gee things up a bit. Shunning an attractive, small-car design from stylist Howard "Dutch" Darrin, Kaiser settled for a no-hoper concept from

unusual fenderline was hard to resist.
The 1950 Mercury illustrated, belongs to Mike Butler of Auburn, who has known this car since his childhood. Previously owned by an old lady who knew of Mike's love for the car, it was passed on to him and remains his treasured possession.

American Metal Products. 1951 was the Henry J's debut and it sold surprisingly well. After the initial spurt it was downhill all the way and production ended in 1954. Bill Arnold's mint Henry J. is a model powered by Kaiser's 161 cu. in. Supersonic six.

Chrome plate and stainless trim were in abundance on GM's 1958 models, the new Chevrolet Bel Air Impala Sport Coupe being no exception. New from the ground up, the Chevrolet had a 117.5 inch wheelbase and a length of 209 inches compared to the '57's 115 and 200 inches. Interiors were attractive in an extrovert sort of way and the steering wheel was supposed to remind you that perhaps a Corvette was in your future. Owned by Mike Triboulet.

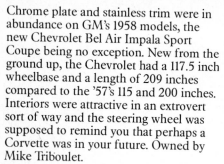

Radio manufacturer Powell Crosley went into the economy car business in 1939. After the war Crosleys sold quite well but innovations like four wheel disc brakes and stamped sheet metal four cylinder engines suffered numerous problems. 1952 was the last year of the Crosley, now with drum brakes and a cast iron four . . . unfortunately nobody wanted econocars in the days when everything big was better. This 1952 car is owned by John E. Nichols, Fla.

A glance at this car, with its continental spare wheel cover, wire wheels and narrow windshield, tells you it must be the ultra expensive 1953 Skylark, built to celebrate Buick's 50th Anniversary.

The Skylark came with every option as standard equipment and cost $4600. The high price put off a lot of buyers and only 1690 units were built. Buick tried again with a smaller version in 1954 and a price reduction of $300. This one only sold 836 units and it was dropped at the end of the year. Of the two versions, the '53 was a far better looking automobile with a level of quality workmanship sadly lacking in today's cars. Although the skylark shared its toothy grin with lesser Buicks, its lines were reasonably free of embellishments and was notable for its lack of "portholes." Ron Lintz is the owner.

The car pictured here is not one of the racing Cunninghams but the 1953 C-3 "production" model. Styled by Michelotti, then working for Vignale, the Italian coachbuilders, the C-3 was one of only two 1953 American cars to be included in the New York Museum of Modern Art's list of the world's Ten Best Cars. Looking at the picture of the car taken on a late Fall evening in Florida, courtesy of the Elliott Museum at Stuart, it's not hard to see why it was picked. Under the hood is the all-powerful Chrysler hemi which turns this sleek grand tourer into a potent piece of transportation.

Not everything that came out of Detroit during the fifties was trimmed to excess. In fact the "creme de la creme" of Chrysler's 1955 crop, the C-300, had extremely clean lines. This beautiful car, styled by Virgil Exner, had a New Yorker body and an Imperial grille but the effect was striking.

The C-300 was a true grand tourer in every sense of the description. It was also the hottest car produced by a U.S. manufacturer, a point soon realised by drivers of rival makes competing in the NASCAR, AAA and Daytona Speedweeks championships. The big, white 300 horsepower chargers won almost everything in sight and became the first and only car to win all three championships at once, thanks to sponsor Carl Kiekhaufer of Mercury Outboard Motors. Our pictures show singer Richard Carpenter's pristine example.

A radical design by Dutch Darrin was marketed by Kaiser as the Kaiser Darrin sportscar in 1954. Based on the Henry J's 100 in. wheelbase and powered by Willys' six cylinder, 90 hp engine, the K.D. was a unique concept. It was built from fiberglass and came with sliding doors and landau top. Tail lights were lifted from the Kaiser Manhattan and the odd grille looked like a pair of pouting lips. The car was quite versatile with a top speed of 100 mph and thrifty, with 30 mpg.

Fred De Vault and William Clark own the car on these pages and it is one of only 435 built before Kaiser went under.

Two Studebakers, three years apart, feature on these pages. The black car is the 1953 model designed by Robert E. Bourke, chief of Loewy's Design Studio. This is a Commander State Regal Hardtop and is powered by Studebaker's 259 cid V-8. Owner Alfred Hadley uses his car for show and daily transportation, hence modern road wheels. The gold and white model is the 1956 Golden Hawk, also designed by Loewy's studio. It was the same body as the '53 but heavily facelifted with the inclusion of a new hood, small, classic style grille and rudimentary fins. Under the hood sat the big 352 cu. in. Packard engine. The car is on display at the A-C-D Museum.

1955 thru 1957 Chevrolets are much sought after by collectors today. One highly prized model is the attractively designed Nomad station wagon, which is conservatively valued at anything between $12,000-$15,000 – when new it cost $2,571. Although much the same as regular Chevies, it was its distinctive roof design that set it apart. The photographs *above and top right* illustrate the differences, including the sloped back pillar and large glass area, very well. This example is the 1957 model belonging to Rick Carroll of Jensen Beach, Fla.

The Billie Joe Spears song, "57 Chevrolet" is a loving tribute to one of the best Chevrolets ever made. Its durability can be attested by its extraordinarily high survival rate. An option on the '57s was the famous 283 cid V-8, rated at 283 hp, or one horsepower per cubic inch. Robert Rodgers is the proud owner of the car pictured *above, top left and facing page.*

Bowing to dealer insistance for a new Continental, Ford produced this Gordon Buehrig, John Reinhart, Bob Thomas design *above and facing page* for 1956. It was unlike anything else on the market and assembly quality approached that of Rolls-Royce, as did the price. Each car cost $10,000 and even then Ford lost $1,000 on each unit sold of this limited production automobile. Sales were disappointing and the Mk. II ended its run in 1957. Bob Edson of Hartford City, Ind., is the proud owner.

Designed in America and built in England to American specifications, the Nash Metropolitan *above and left*, brainchild of Nash president George Mason, went on sale in 1954. 83,422 cars later, the Metro ended its eight year run, a victim of Detroit's compact boom. Stylist Bill Flajole and engineer Meade Moore were the true creators of the Metropolitan. Austin of England was contracted to assemble the car using Austin's four cylinder A-40 engine, transmission and modified suspension parts. In 1956 the engine was enlarged from 70 to 90 cid. Because there was no trunk lid until 1959, the spare wheel was carried continental fashion at the rear. Vernon D. Crews owns this mint 1957 example.

Arguably the most attractive of the three year cycle of two seater Thunderbirds was the 1957 model, shown here. Slightly longer than the 1955/56 models, the last two seat T-Bird had modest tailfins flanking the lengthened trunk area. A combined front bumper/grille treatment worked commendably well. Retained from 1956 was the optional bolt-on hardtop complete with glass "portholes" which was light enough for one man operation. This fine specimen is on show at the A-C-D Museum, Auburn, Ind.

It looked like a car, it rode like a car but there the similarity ended. In 1957 Ford announced a new vehicle; the Ranchero half-ton pickup. Pickups had been around for a long time but they looked like small trucks. The Ranchero combined the best of both worlds providing utility with style. The beautiful red and white example above, belongs to Bill Arnold of Petersburg, Ind., and has Ford's 223 cu. in. Mileage Maker Six under the hood.

If ever there was a car that epitomised the flamboyant fifties then Ford's Skyliner Retractable Hardtop has to be a strong contender for the crown. The steel top was originally meant for the 1956 Continental Mk. II but was ultimately developed by Ford and appeared on the Skyliner in 1957. The roof mechanism consisted of five motors, 13 switches, 10 solenoids, nine circuit breakers and 610 feet of wiring. When the "retract" switch is moved, the front section of the roof folds under and the top gracefully begins its descent into the oversize trunk. Delbert Fellers has owned this pristine example from new. *Overleaf, left* a 1966 Chrysler 300 convertible, owned by Wayne E. Boyd of Auburn, Ind. *Overleaf, right* the compact Ford Falcon, introduced in 1960 and powered by a 170 ci six, outsold the opposition all the way down the line.

The $250 million certainty that failed is one way of describing the luckless Edsel. Launched in 1958 to bolster Ford's mid-price range, the Edsel was supposed to take away sales from GM and Chrysler's medium price cars. Nearly ten years of research went into the Edsel and included an intense market survey, the results of which augured well for a new mid-priced automobile. Sadly, the market research people were way off course. A publicity campaign designed to whet consumers' appetites was the only thing to succeed about the Edsel. It gave the impression that the Edsel was radically different from anything that had gone before. So it was with great disappointment that prospective customers viewed the Edsel for the first time. It was utterly conventional save the vertical "horse-collar" grille and automatic shift buttons set in the steering wheel hub.

The Edsel couldn't have been launched at a worse time. 1958 was the Eisenhower recession year and medium-price car sales slumped alarmingly. Three years later the Edsel was no more.

The pictures show the slightly cleaned up 1959 Ranger model equipped with the 303 bhp V-8. The car belongs to Denis Winebrenner, Auburn, Ind.

①

②

③

④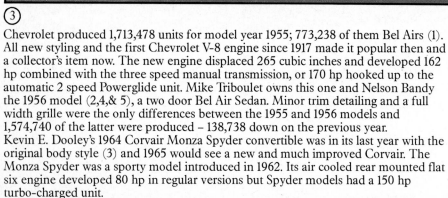

Chevrolet produced 1,713,478 units for model year 1955; 773,238 of them Bel Airs (1). All new styling and the first Chevrolet V-8 engine since 1917 made it popular then and a collector's item now. The new engine displaced 265 cubic inches and developed 162 hp combined with the three speed manual transmission, or 170 hp hooked up to the automatic 2 speed Powerglide unit. Mike Triboulet owns this one and Nelson Bandy the 1956 model (2,4,& 5), a two door Bel Air Sedan. Minor trim detailing and a full width grille were the only differences between the 1955 and 1956 models and 1,574,740 of the latter were produced – 138,738 down on the previous year.

Kevin E. Dooley's 1964 Corvair Monza Spyder convertible was in its last year with the original body style (3) and 1965 would see a new and much improved Corvair. The Monza Spyder was a sporty model introduced in 1962. Its air cooled rear mounted flat six engine developed 80 hp in regular versions but Spyder models had a 150 hp turbo-charged unit.

It started out as a Thunderbird but after Ford president, Robert McNamara saw the designs and said it should be the new Lincoln Continental, that is what it became. Launched in 1961, the new Continental was as different from its over-ornate predecessor as chalk is from cheese. It was also unique in many ways; being the only four door convertible model available anywhere, the doors opening from the center.

Tooling forward of the cowl was shared with Thunderbird to cut costs, though you couldn't tell.
The Continental's headlight bezels, joined by a chrome bar across the middle of the grille, are a styling feature almost identical to the '61 T-Bird. Dorothy and Jerry Coburn own this excellent example and use it for long distance travelling vacations.

Bill Mitchell designed it, Zora Arkus Duntov engineered it and the result was the 1963 Corvette Stingray shown here. The semi-boat tail rear, novel split rear window design and pivoting, hidden headlights caused a sensation in motoring circles throughout the world. With its all round independent suspension, choice of engines and fuel injection, the fiberglass bodied Stingray was a match for most European sportscars, even more so with the addition of four wheel disc brakes in 1965. Offered as a coupe and convertible, the Stingray met with immediate public acceptance to the tune of 21,000 produced, some 7000 up on the previous model.

Auburn, Ind. dentist Mike Hayes, spotted this Stingray for sale at a Kruse auction. The car didn't sell, fortunately for Mr. Hayes, who haggled a price and became the Stingray's new owner.

The breathtaking 1963 Riviera Sport Coupe was Buick's entry into the Thunderbird dominated "personal luxury" car market. Its razor-edged design was unlike anything else produced by GM, possessing an elegance and poise that set it apart from the

rest. The Riviera was pure artistry on wheels, thanks to the gifted William L. Mitchell who blended a subtle mix of European and American influences to create a true classic. This example belongs to Larry K. Riesen, Fort Wayne, Ind.

1966 was the Mustang's second year and sales went up to over 600,000. Best selling model was the hardtop equipped with the 289 cu. in. V-8. Over 56,000 convertibles were built, like the '66 model shown. The engine is the 289. The chromed pony, set in the recessed grille, coined the name used to describe a host of similar... ponycars! The standard buckets were quite comfortable and instruments reasonably legible. Lindsey Goodman of Auburn, Indiana, is the car's proud owner. *Overleaf, left* a 1967 Pontiac GTO, one of the fastest cars of the decade, with a 0-60 time of under 5 seconds. *Overleaf, right* Chrysler's musclecar: the Plymouth Belvedere GTX of 1968.

All the hoopla that went with the Judge – no doubt inspired by the Plymouth Roadrunner – disguised its true place in the musclecar scheme. It entered the fray in 1969, rather late in the day, as it happened. Not that this mattered unduly; it had, after all, the GTO's wealth of experience behind it.

Never mind the dainty pink stripes, everything worked. The hood scoops, the hood mounted tach, all were functional. Under the hood throbbed 400 cubic inches of Ram-Air engine which knocked up 0 – 60 times in little over 6 seconds.

Up front was Pontiac's rubbery Endura covered bumper painted the same color as the body. Combined with white lettered tires and mag-style wheels the Judge looked the part it meant to play.

The car shown belongs to Don Andrews.

This is a Ford that meant business, a car not to be treated lightly; a Shelby Cobra Mustang GT 500. From the beginning, Ford handed Carroll Shelby their Mustangs for him to perform his magic and turn them into stiff handling, gut churning automobiles. Ford, very much into its Total Performance kick, considered Shelby Mustangs good image makers. With Shelby's extensive modifications these Mustangs, especially the GT 500 model, could outperform their competitors. The pictures show Stephen R. Keusch's venomous Cobra GT 500. Functional air scoops abound, and to reduce the weight the hood is of fiberglass. Seating was stock Mustang, but the mahogany rim steering wheel and comprehensive instrumentation were unique to Shelby.

Chevrolet's Camaro arrived on the motoring scene a little more than two years after Ford's successful Mustang. Launched at the same time as near-identical twin, Pontiac's Firebird, Chevrolet initially dished up the impressive Z/28 option for racing use. In this guise, the Camaro beat factory backed Mustangs in the last two races of the 1967 Trans-Am season, followed by a first and second in the Trans-Am class in the 12 hour 1968 Sebring event. The 1969 Z/28 shown here, has the small block 302 cid V-8. Zero to 60 with the 302 was slightly over 7 seconds but the standing quarter, according to road tests, was a phenomenal 14.85 at 101.4 mph. This example belongs to the A-C-D Museum, Auburn, Ind. *Overleaf* the Skyliner convertible hardtop.

Copyright ©1988 by Colour Library Books Ltd.,
Guildford, Surrey, England.
First published in USA 1988
by Exeter Books
Distributed by Bookthrift
Exeter is a trademark of Bookthrift Marketing, Inc.
Bookthrift is a registered trademark of Bookthrift Marketing, Inc.
New York, New York

ISBN 0–671–09398–3

Printed in Spain by Cronion, S.A.